Color Me
LOVE

Color Me Love

13-Digit ISBN: 978-1-64643-303-2
10-Digit ISBN: 1-64643-303-3

This book may be ordered by mail from the publisher. Please include $5.99 for postage and handling. Please support your local bookseller first!

Books published by Cider Mill Press Book Publishers are available at special discounts for bulk purchases in the United States by corporations, institutions, and other organizations. For more information, please contact the publisher.

Cider Mill Press Book Publishers
"Where Good Books Are Ready for Press"
501 Nelson Place
Nashville, TN 37214

cidermillpress.com

Printed in the United States

Typography: Epicursive Script, Filson Pro

23 24 25 26 27 VER 7 6 5 4 3

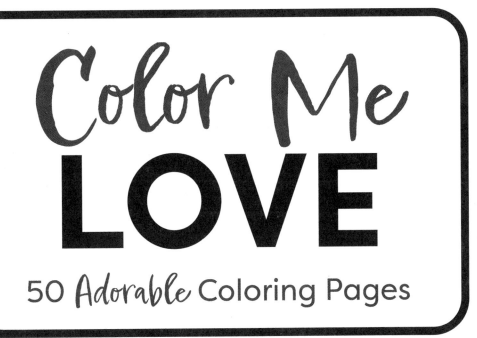

Color Me LOVE

50 Adorable Coloring Pages

Illustrations by Natalie Briscoe

CIDER MILL PRESS

BOOK PUBLISHERS

Introduction

If you're reading this, you're our kind of person. Maybe you're stressed out from work or exhausted by your social life—or maybe you just love love! For whatever reason, you've decided to unwind with this adorable adult coloring book. You've chosen the right activity; coloring books are proven to reduce anxiety and lift negative moods.

These delightful designs are suitable for all skill levels. The pages are one-sided, so your art won't bleed through. You can use whatever tool you want to fill in these charming illustrations: colored pencils, markers, gel pens, watercolors, crayons, you name it. Color inside the lines or outside of them—the point is to relax and create something that makes you happy.

These detailed illustrations allow you to practice mindfulness and will keep you busy for hours. You can enjoy the meditative benefits in silence, or maybe you'd like to curate a different kind of calming atmosphere with some music. You can even invite a friend to color with you; this book makes a great gift.

However you choose to bring these coloring pages to life, we're sure that you'll enjoy unleashing your inner artist with these beautiful illustrations. Share your enchanting creations with the world by posting on social media with the hashtag #colormelove (and be sure to tag us @cidermillpress)! Now go forth and find your bliss with *Color Me Love*.

The world can be an ugly place. Brighten it up with flying cupids, cuddly animals, candy hearts, and more! Life got you stressed out? Take some time for yourself. Focus on the journey, not the destination, as you explore the intricate detail of these stunning illustrations. The destination will be satisfying no matter how you get there! Frame your masterpieces to beautify your own space, or bring joy to that special someone by gifting them your charming creations. Now open up to any page—it's time to add some color to your day!

Share Your
MASTERPIECES

Don't keep your colorful creations to yourself—take a pic and share it on social media with the hashtag **#colormelove** and tag us @cidermillpress!

#COLORMELOVE #COLORMELOVE
#COLORMELOVE #COLORMELOVE
#COLORMELOVE #COLORMELOVE
#COLORMELOVE #COLORMELOVE
#COLORMELOVE #COLORMELOVE
#COLORMELOVE #COLORMELOVE
#COLORMELOVE #COLORMELOVE
#COLORMELOVE #COLORMELOVE
#COLORMELOVE #COLORMELOVE
#COLORMELOVE #COLORMELOVE
#COLORMELOVE #COLORMELOVE
#COLORMELOVE #COLORMELOVE
#COLORMELOVE #COLORMELOVE
#COLORMELOVE #COLORMELOVE
#COLORMELOVE #COLORMELOVE
#COLORMELOVE #COLORMELOVE
#COLORMELOVE #COLORMELOVE
#COLORMELOVE #COLORMELOVE
#COLORMELOVE #COLORMELOVE
#COLORMELOVE #COLORMELOVE
#COLORMELOVE #COLORMELOVE
#COLORMELOVE #COLORMELOVE
#COLORMELOVE #COLORMELOVE

About
CIDER MILL PRESS
BOOK PUBLISHERS

Good ideas ripen with time. From seed to harvest,
Cider Mill Press brings fine reading, information, and
entertainment together between the covers of its creatively
crafted books. Our Cider Mill bears fruit twice a year,
publishing a new crop of titles each spring and fall.

"Where Good Books Are Ready for Press"

501 Nelson Place
Nashville, TN 37214

cidermillpress.com